For my family. I love you dearly.

Thank you for your help, encouragement and

patience in making a childhood dream become reality!

Copyright © 2018 by Matthew A. Lapides

All rights reserved.

Without limiting the rights under copyright reserved alone, no part of this book may be reproduced or transmitted in any form or by any means, electronic or mechanical, including photocopying, recording, or by any information storage and retrieval system, without prior written permission of both the copyright owner and the publisher of this book.

ISBN: 978-0-9995510-9-7

First Edition January 2018
10 9 8 7 6 5 4 3 2 1

Sprout Publishing, LLC
3109 Grand Avenue, #261 • Coconut Grove, FL 33133

www.sproutpublishing.com

Foreword

I was foraging through a stack of boxes in a storage unit I rent, it's really a graveyard for lost memories. I keep telling myself to stop paying to store this "stuff", but my subconscious must be convincing me that those things are priceless and sentimental heirlooms. I really don't know what's in that sacred resting place anymore, just things that don't fit in a house that are not easily disposed.

I opened a box full of books, photo albums and saw an unlabeled composition notebook. I reached for that notebook. It seemed familiar, almost from a dream, but certainly from a time long bygone. With a great surprise, I discovered my old "Book of Lists".

Family break from boat building… on a boat ride! Annapolis, MD. August 2016

What a find! These are lists of things that I would write when I was younger and quite a bit more ambitious. I remembered all the lists that were inside such as "Places I want to visit", "Skills I want to master", and "Things I want to do when I grow up" (I really thought that I was going to grow up?). A smile grew on my face while I looked at my unexpected time capsule. I sat down and flipped through my youthful aspirations, my adult eyes beamed at the words.

Building a boat can be fatiguing. We took a vacation together, and got a little crabby on this day. Cantler's Riverside Inn, Annapolis, MD. August 2016.

As it turns out, I set my course many years ago, or created a self-fulfilling prophesy. Some items from "Want I want to do when I grow up" included; be a master juggler, learn magic, be a great musician, write a book and build a boat. Building a boat? Yep. This long lost treasure, my book of lists, had been hidden for years or decades.

When the stars of the universe aligned, and the thought of building a boat became a possibility after seeing a demonstration boat build during Miami Sailing Week 2016, I said "Let's build a boat". Now I know that it was somehow already my destiny. I wrote it down as a kid, and now, it was just going to happen. The fruits of my labor are much sweeter, because "we" built a boat, and that dream became a reality. Perhaps that ambition still is flickering, or perhaps it was rekindled.

Everyone has landmarks of triumph, and this is one of ours. Here's what happened during the Summer of 2016 in our Ipanema Villa garage in Coconut Grove, Florida.

March 12, 2016. 68 days to commencement.

Meet George.

He made us curious.

Everything has a beginning. In this case, we were motivated by watching this fellow, George, who was building a small boat during Miami Sailing Week 2016 in Coconut Grove. We watched his progress every day for a week... even a few times a day. George spent his days as chemist for NASA in Cape Canaveral, FL, and spends free time designing and building boats. He is a master builder, quite a nice man and helped us out with terrific building tips along our odyssey.

March 14, 2016. 66 days before commencement.

He inspired us.

I think I can, I think I can… George showed me a catalogue of boat kits as a starting point. There were lots of choices, and the thought of making a boat invigorated me in an unexpectedly curious way. It seems like I had envisioned myself doing this for a long time. This image came from a time-lapse camera that took pictures every 5 minutes at the build hut in CocoWalk. Bing!

March 16, 2016. 64 days before commencement.

He encouraged us.

**Decision made.
All thumbs up for building a boat... done!**

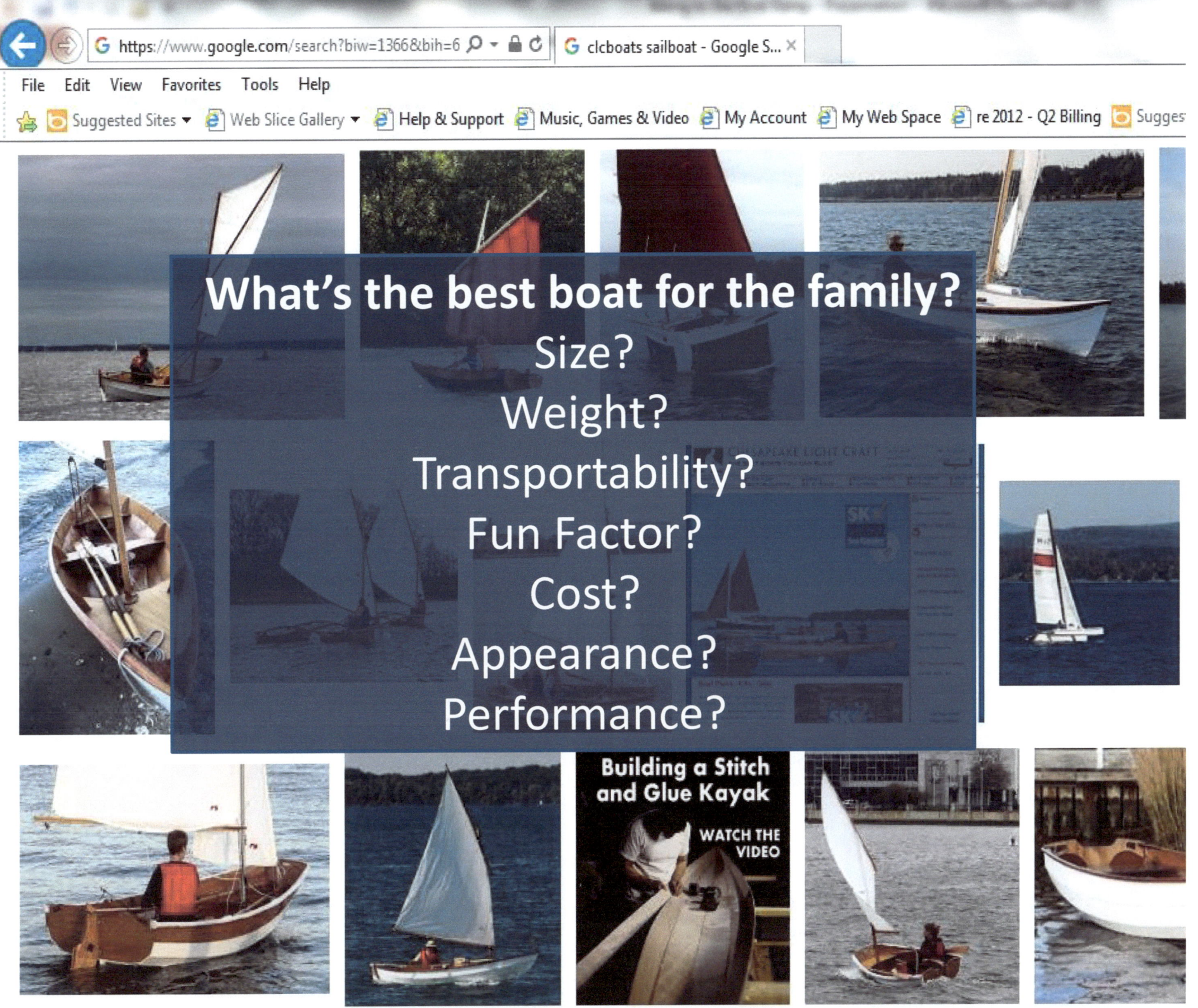

Final Choice:

Northeaster Dory

Length: 17' 0"
Beam: 56"
Rowing Draft: 5"
Sailing Draft: 24"
Hull Weight: 100 lbs
Rigged Weight: 120 lbs
Max Payload: 800 lbs
Sail Area: 68 sq ft

- 150 year old design
- Narrow waterline
- Flared topside
- Great load carrier
- Fast Hull
- Sloop or Lug rig
- Sail or row
- Lots of Boat!

Can you build a 17' boat fit in a 17½' deep garage?
Let's find out… Here we go!

Day 1, May 20, 2016 – Delivery Day

These are boxes.

The stuff inside is full of potential, but right now, it's just a bunch of wood feeling a bit strapped.

The Beginning

Day 2

This is a boy. He is also full of potential but doesn't know it yet. He just unstrapped a box and released great potential.

It may be simple, but today we learned to cut away from your body when you open a box with a sharp knife. That little lesson will help me worry less about my son, and help him stay a bit safer in life. Perhaps he will pass along some of these simple but smart lessons to those that he will care for someday.

Day 2 - Inside a box of wood

Okoume Wood — A relative of mahogany and a native to the Congo in Africa. Okoume is known to be incredibly strong, but lightweight. The wood for this boat has already been around the world; it was grown on a farm in Africa, finished in France, laser cut in Annapolis, MD, and trucked to Miami, FL. What a trip to get to us! Now, let's see what the pieces make together.

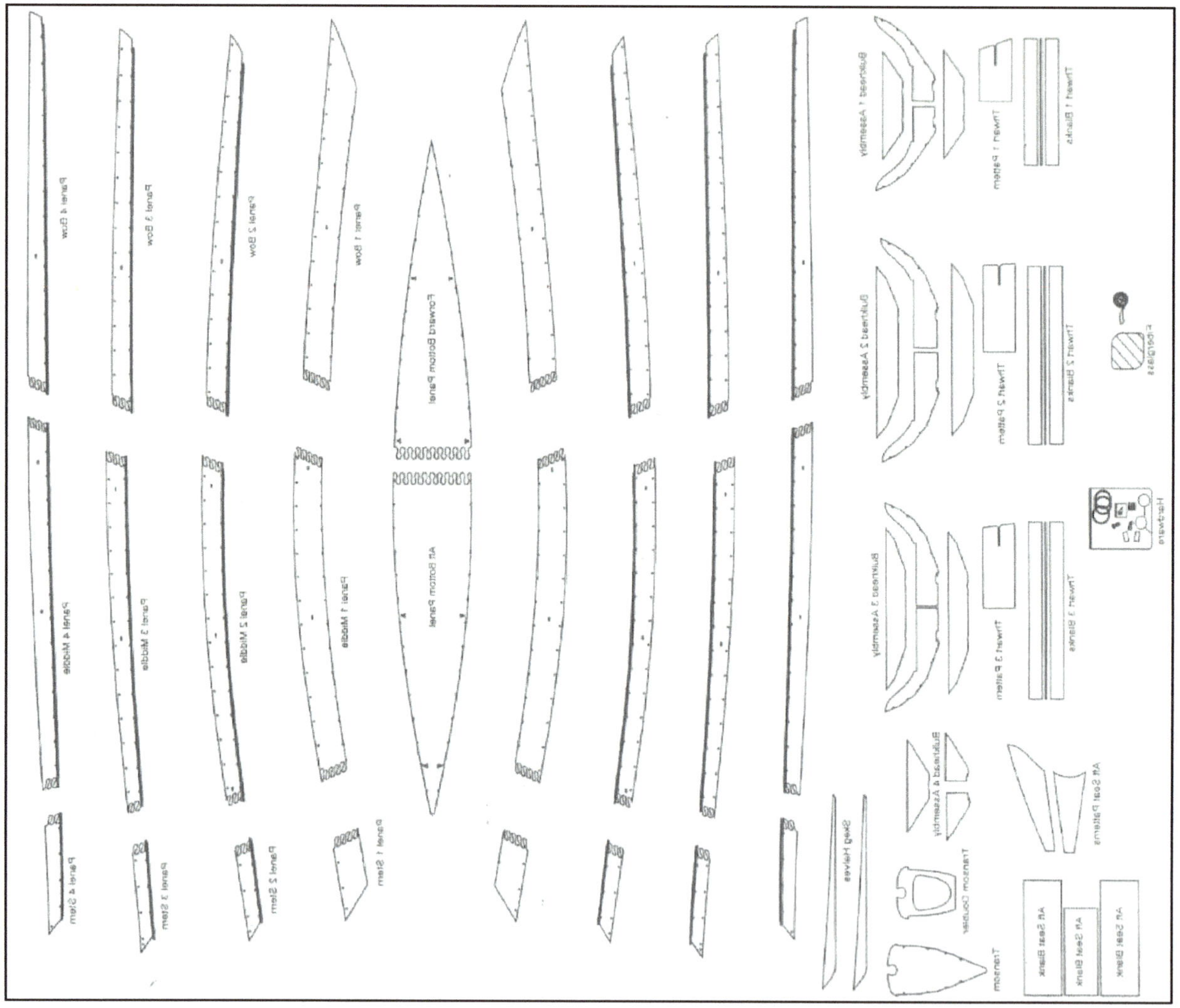

These are the shapes of wood that we found in the box.

Day 5 – Pre-assembly

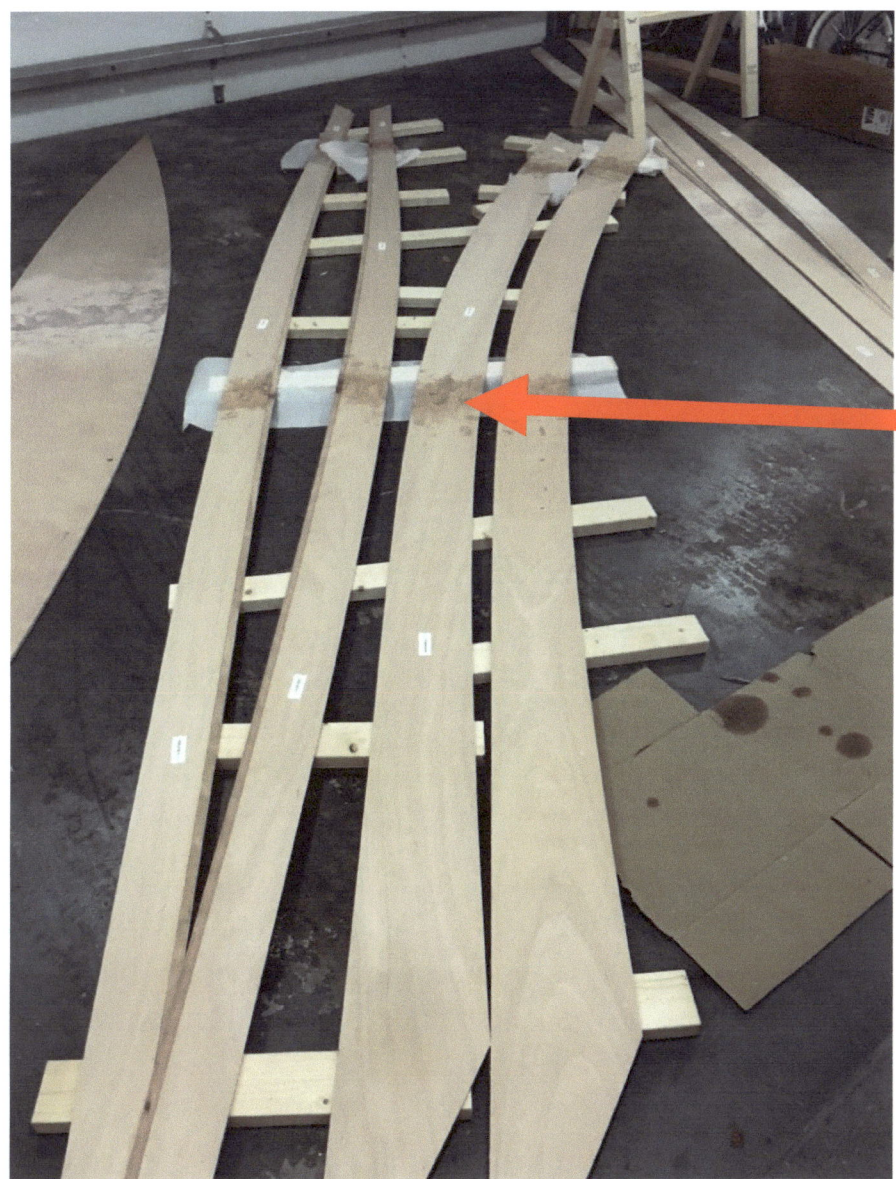

Puzzle joints

A chain is only as strong as its weakest link.

These "puzzle" joints had to be connected to make the side panels. Oops, how long are these things? A 17' boat has a curved side, so the panels are much longer than 17' when straight. The garage is only 17.5' long, uh-oh! Looks like our first lesson, but we're resilient!

Day 8 - Play it Safe

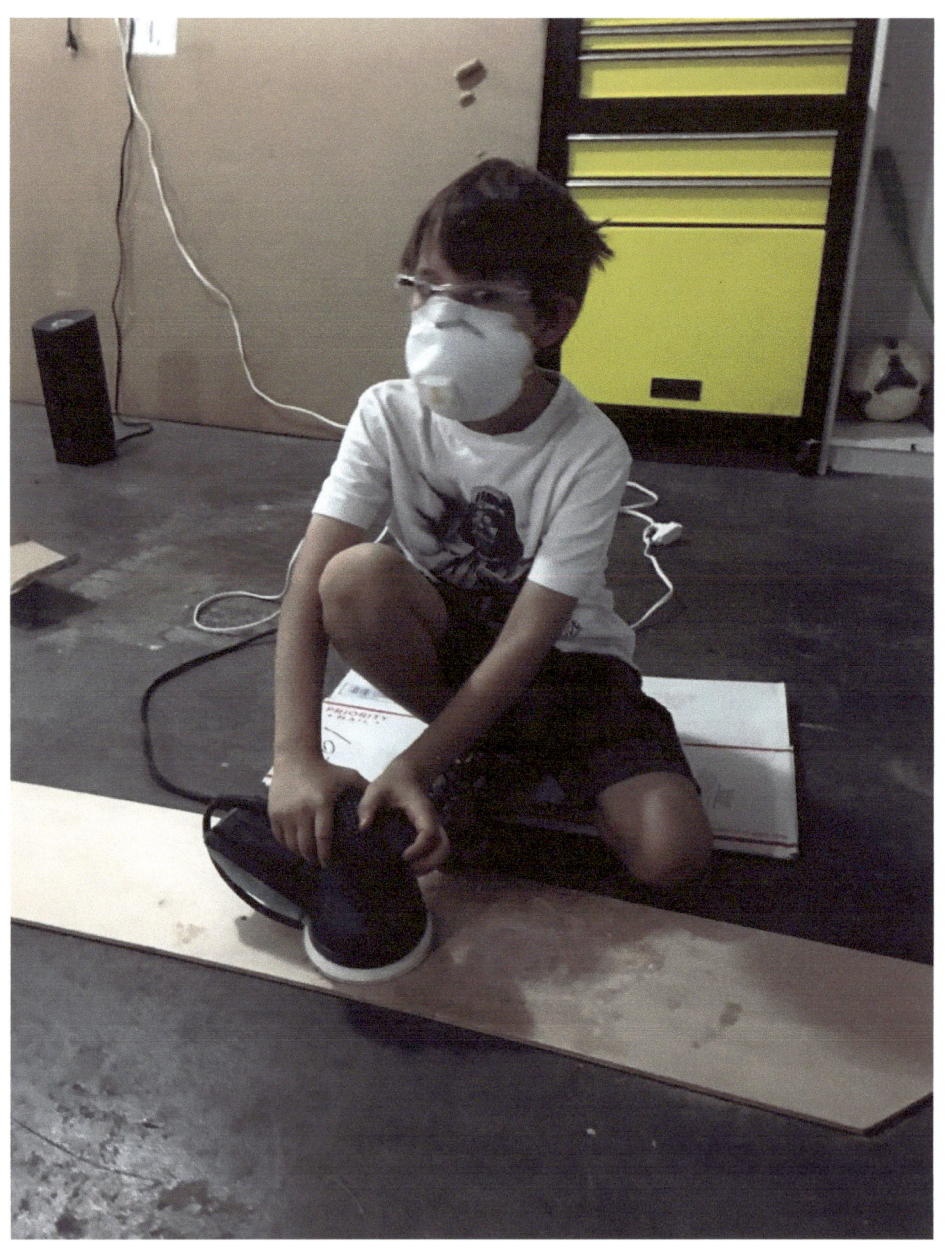

Know safety, no injury.
No safety, know injury.

To learn about eye protection, ask someone who has one.

Don't learn safety by accident.

Sometimes, the best way to learn something, is by doing it. Young man Ethan jumped right in. He learned how to use some pretty cool tools to makes important parts for the boat, but he also learned safety first.

Woodworking requires patience, and with great care, this young man made perfectly smooth puzzle joints.

Day 9 - Taking Shape

Before the reward, there must be labor.

You plant before you harvest.

You sow in tears before you reap joy.

The shape of the boat comes together quickly. At this point, we are proud builders and a bit naïve about the work ahead of us. A boat takes shape quickly, that's the easy part.

This lady sits upon a pair of wooden I-beam shaped horses that offer plenty of area to clamp. We built these wooden horses to the right "family height" to hold the hull and allow everyone to work at the right height.

Day 12 – Look, a boat!

The hair of a man's beard is as tough as the same size copper wire.

Copper wire holds the boat together... Hundreds of them! With some measuring and a few twists fore and aft, the boat is properly shaped and leveled before permanent epoxy work is applied.

Day 19, June 5 – The Pastry Chef

Success is the sum of details.

Every seam matters. Epoxy was mixed with an additive for strength and placed into a freezer bag. It looked like pastry filling. We snip the corner of the bag, and squeezed epoxy into all of the over-lapping seams. This holds the boat together, gives strength, and keeps the boat light. This takes quite a bit of time to seal all of the panels from the outside.

Day 20, June 8

Wood flour feels as soft as confectioners sugar, but becomes as strong as steel with the right mix.

All of those copper wire are removed. For those wires that were epoxied in place, we heat the copper with a soldering iron for a moment, and the wire slides right out of the wood.

Using a large wooden "tongue depressor", we epoxy all interior corners for strength while paying attention to a clean installation. After all, this has to be functional and beautiful! The other seams of the boat had another additive white powder called "Cell-o-Fill" to thicken the epoxy and provide additional strength.

Day 23, June 11

The rewards for those who persevere far exceed the pain that must precede the victory.

This boat only needs fiberglass on the bottom and lower panel for strength. This is "wetting down" the fiberglass; the fabric is soaked with epoxy and the excess is pressed out. Watch for bubbles, they will weaken the hull. When Renata was pouring the epoxy into the boat, she asked, "You mixed this, right?". My heart stopped. A hundred thoughts sped through my brain on how to fix this unmixed mess. She gave me a sneer... oh, she got me good with late night boat humor. Building a boat in a garage: Awesome. Building a boat in the garage at midnight with Renata, my Brazilian Barbie: PRICELESS. I should marry her, wait, I did!

Day 26, June 14

She's taking shape with skillful hands, a protected face and an orbital sander.

Vvvvvvvvrrrrrrrrr!

Every last inch, inside and out, gets sanded as she takes shape into a seaworthy vessel. The museum quality appearance we seek is a result of care at every step. We pay attention to every little inch.

Day 34 – Becoming Resourceful

Having the right tool for the job makes life much easier!

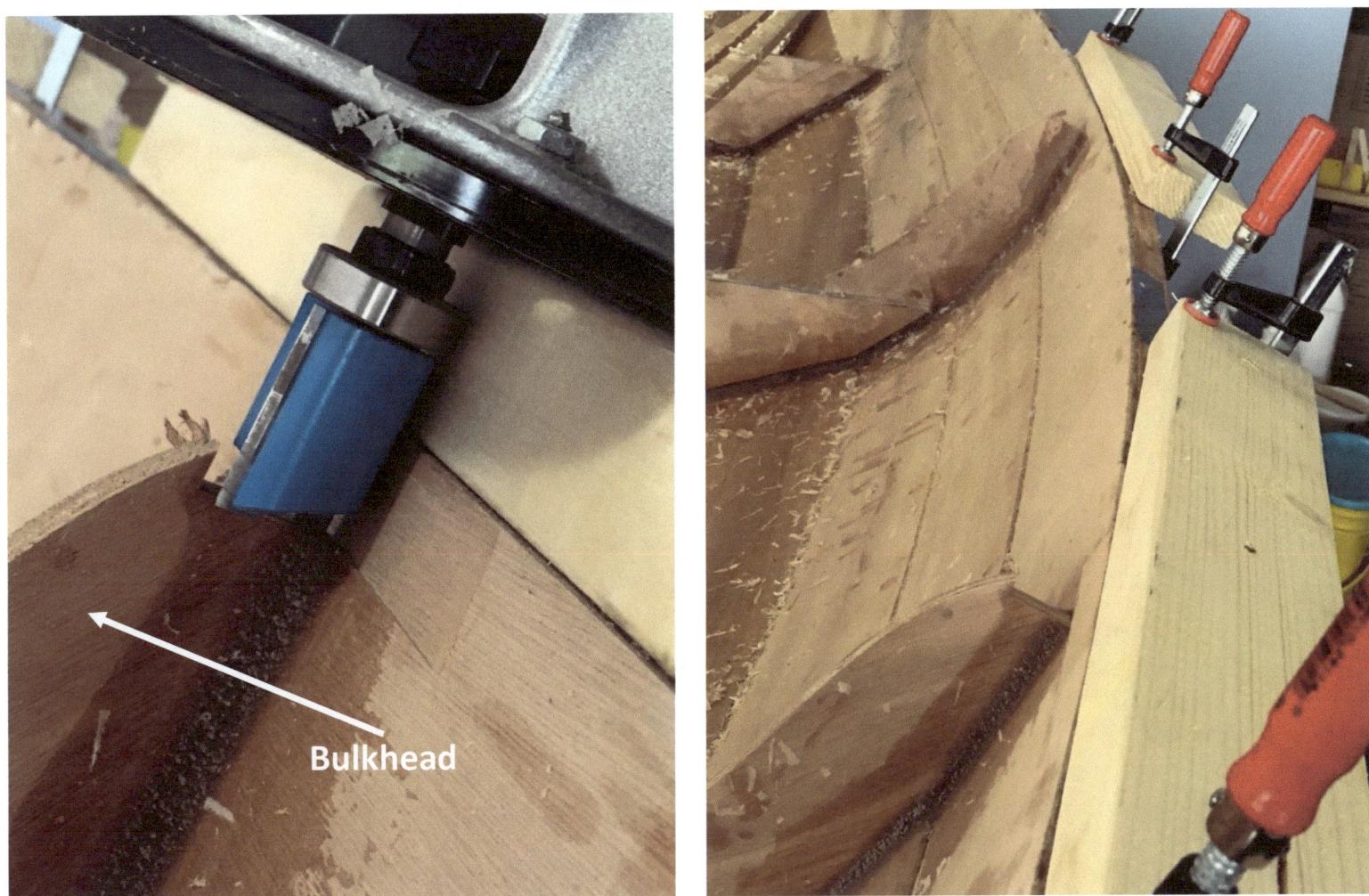

Bulkhead

Remember, measure twice, cut once... really!

We wanted this beauty to stand out, and had to retrofit the boat to install an inner rail (inwale) with spacers in addition to the two outer rail (outwale). We were careful to cut the bulkheads with a router for a nice clean fit and clamped some extra wood as guides to get straight cuts. We were fortunate to find a cabinetry shop with extra tools, and made great use of those finds!

Days 36-45. You can't rush beauty.

Outwale 1

Outwale 1&2 + Inwale Spacers

Inexpensive spring clamps fit on the outwale, but when we added the inwale spacers, we had to move up to bigger clamps (lots and lots of them) for the extra width to clamp down. Thanks again to that cabinet shop that happened to have buckets full of extra clamps. We were saved!

Day 47 – Time to Shine

We are connecting wood in a way that provides function, stability, purpose and hopefully....

One by one, my great helper removed the clamps holding 4 railing layers together. We hoped that everything stayed in place. It did! The excess epoxy that squeezed out made me a bit concerned. However, thanks to some new tools, we were about to be amazed!

Day 48, July 6

... beauty

It took about two weeks to design, cut, sand and epoxy all of the inwale spacer pieces for the inner railing (inwale).

We designed the spacer appearance to maintain the same spacing while also providing locations for 3 sets of oar risers. You can see the three locations easily as marked where there is a solid base.

This oar configuration allows this beauty to be a single (center thwart) or double (fore and aft thwarts) row boat.

There are 4 layers of railings in all. It took merely 5 minutes with a belt sander to expose the beauty of weeks of work. This is getting exciting! What a great day... progress is a strong motivator!

Day 51, July 9 – Half way there

Challenges are what make life interesting.
Overcoming them is what makes life meaningful.

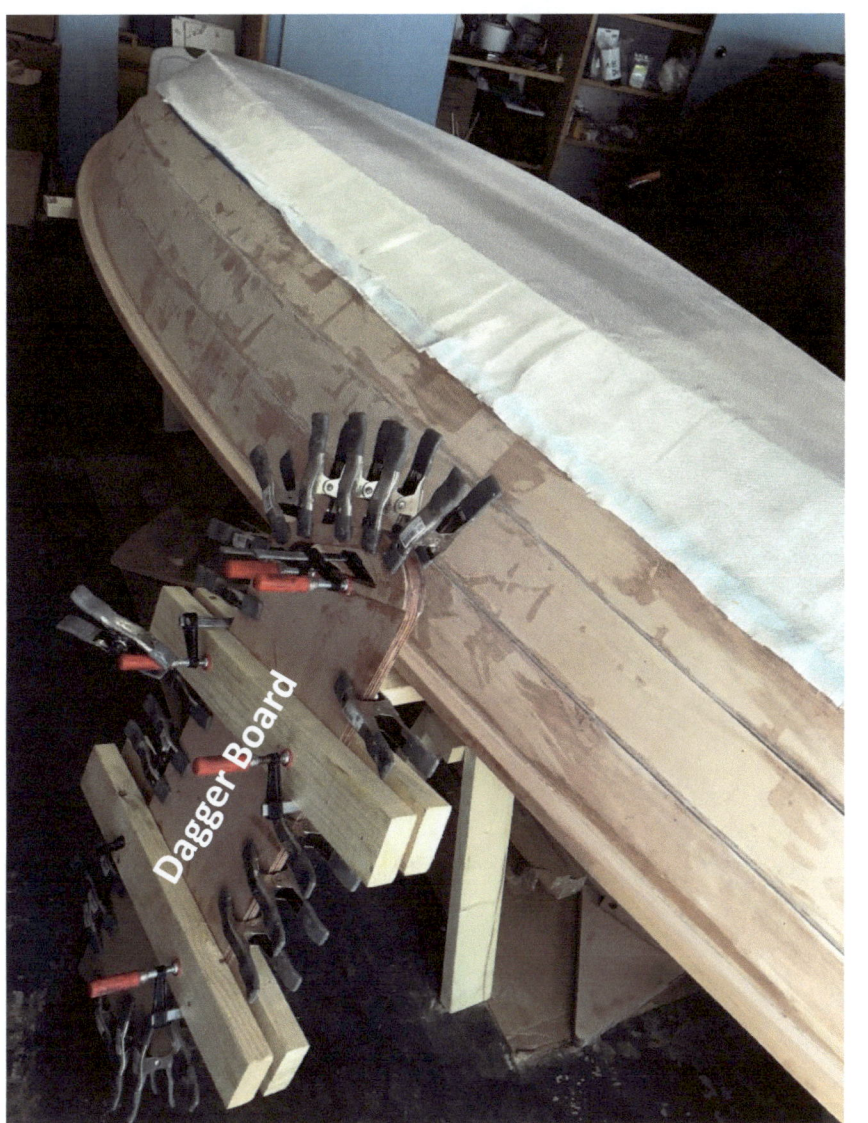

The boat only gets fiberglass from the first railing down, inside and out. We cut the fabric to the right size, and then "wet down" the fiberglass to make a solid and waterproof seal on the bottom. It also protects the wood from scrapes. The daggerboard also takes shape.

Day 54 – Wow, this girl is bright

Epoxy,
Sand,
Repeat.

Epoxy,
Sand,
Repeat.

Epoxy,
Sand,
Repeat.

The final quality of the boat finish is up to the builder. To make the boat look just a little bit nicer takes a lot more work! Epoxy, sand and repeat. This takes days and days and days and days.

Day 56 – She needs love, lots of it

A bad day woodworking is better than a good day working.

The thwarts, or bench seats, are cut, assembled and shaped to fit over the bulkheads. A small support is shaped and epoxied in the hull to receive and firmly hold each thwart.

Day 79 – Are we there yet?

The rewards for those who persevere far exceed the pain that must precede the victory.

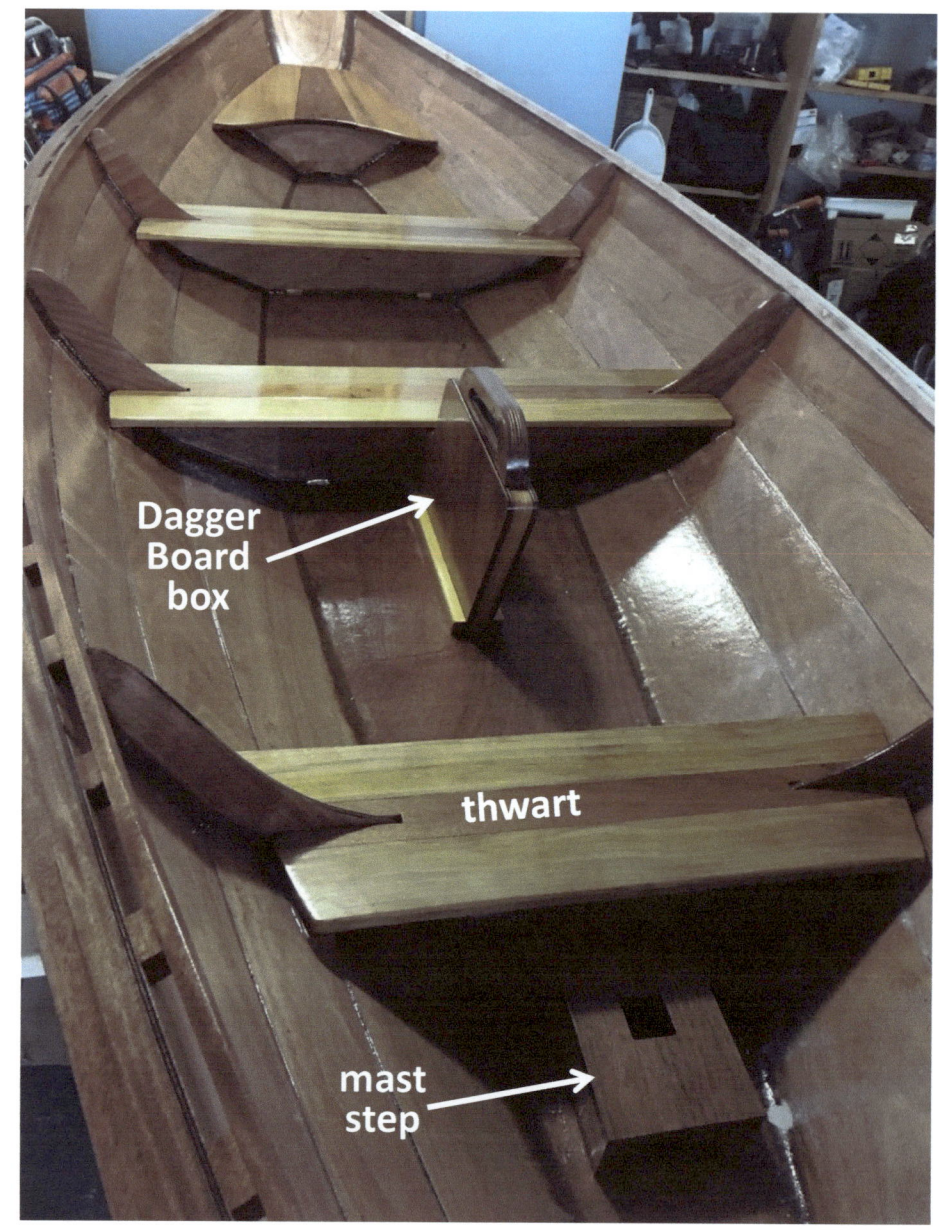

The dagger board box is in place in the center of the boat, the thwarts (seats) are positioned, and the mast step is epoxied in place to receive the mast. Cutting a straight hole for the dagger board box in a perfectly good boat was a bit unnerving. If it is at an angle facing port or starboard, she would have a tough time sailing upwind on one side, or do circles. If the box is not vertical, she will have some drift when you sail. I think we got it nice and square with the use of several braces.

Day 97 – Resilience conquers fatigue

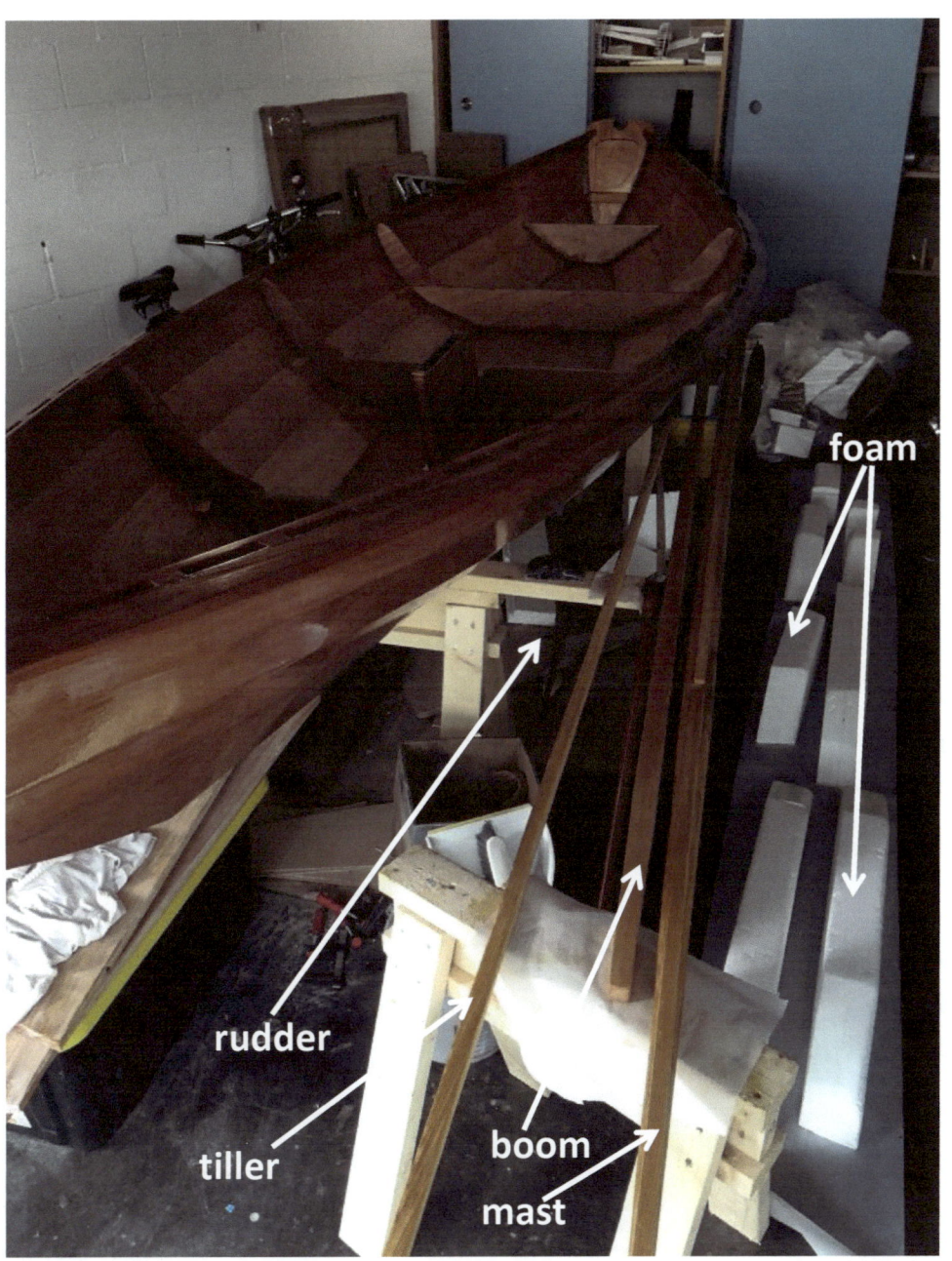

Notice the open storage door in the back. We needed every inch we could find!

Anybody can become a woodworker, but only a Craftsmen can hide his mistakes!

There are lots of other parts besides the hull when you build a boat. We have been building for over 3 months, and these other parts take plenty of time to shape and prepare:

Mast: This 20 foot piece of wood holds up the sails. The mast starts in 2 parts, it is epoxied together with a scarf joint and shaped carefully. The 4"x4" mast gets shaped to be less than 1" x 1" at the top.

Boom: Attaches to the mast and holds the bottom of the sail. The boom is also rounded.

Rudder: Steers the boat. Several parts.

Tiller: A long pole attached to the rudder to steer from anywhere inside the cockpit.

Foam Flotation: Layers of foam are sandwiched together, cut and shaped to fit under the thwarts. They add important flotation to the boat in a discreet fashion.

Day 117 – The final countdown

First passenger ever!

Still under construction.

Beauty takes time, a really really, really long time.

Target date for the maiden voyage is just 5 days away. Every hour counts!

Renata is not only great at fiberglass, she knows quite a bit about style and design. Instead of epoxy painting the white foam blocks, she suggested to cover the foam with caning, a woven bamboo material often used for chairs.

That idea took an extra week or more to incorporate. The caning had to be properly cut, epoxied in place on the foam and coated with varnish to protect it from the sun. Wow, what a great tropical addition!

Day 119, September 14

Target date for Maiden Voyage is 3 days away. Crunch time. Paint. Wet sand. Paint. Wet sand. Paint. Wet sand.

My helpers are versatile and amazing! Renata can fiberglass, design, paint, and bring the right food and drink at exactly the right time at almost any time of day. And, that's just the beginning. The summer heat was a challenge with the epoxy and paint. Keeping those materials in air conditioning before use allowed use more time to apply these things before they began to set-up.

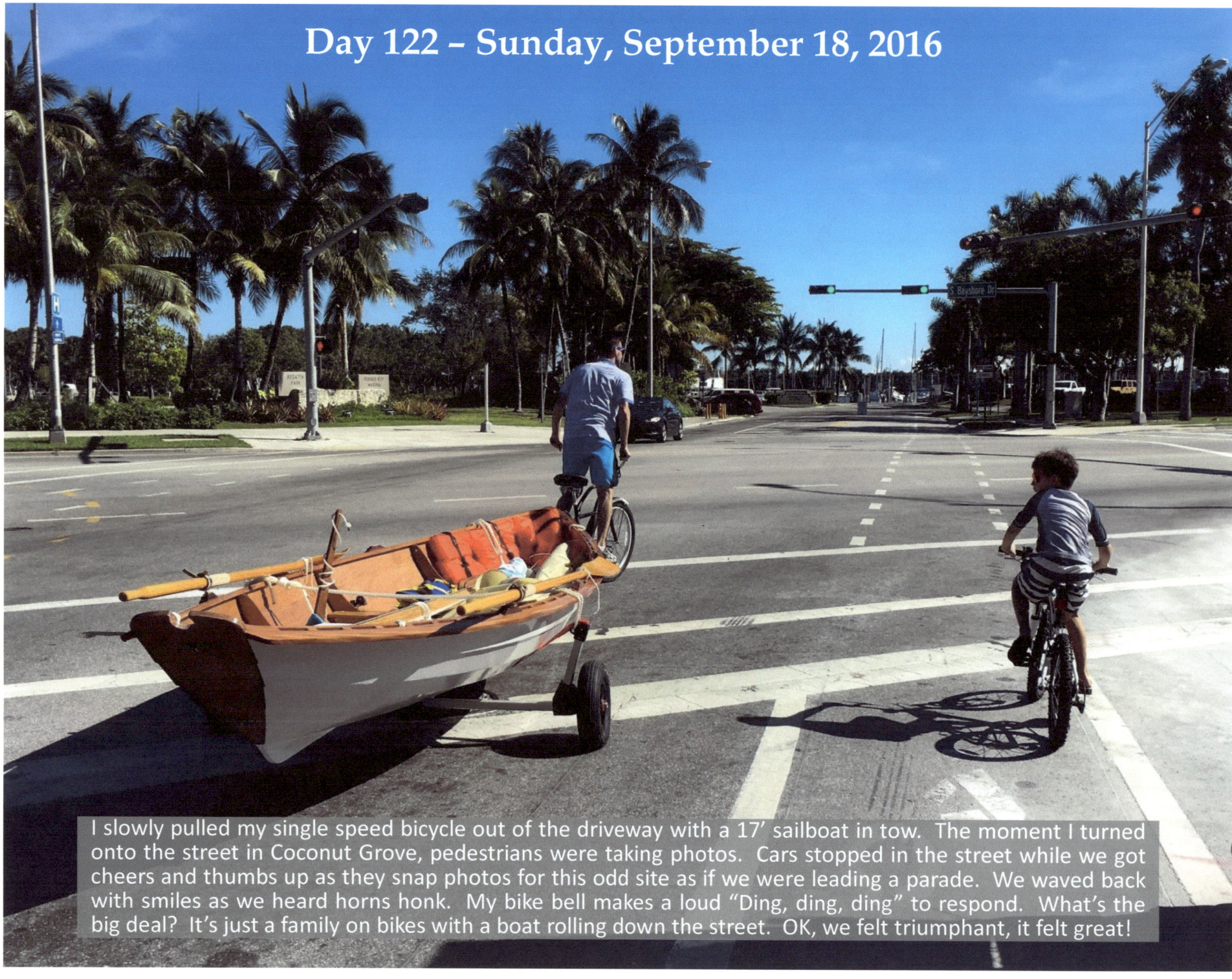

Every project has challenges, and every project has its rewards.

Day 122, September 18, 2016

The Reward.

Introducing "MARE". Each letter of MARE comes from the first letter of the first names of our family build team. In Portuguese, "mare" means "tides".

We're pretty sure that this is what hard work and patience looks like.

The rudder is built to "pop-up" if it runs aground.   The red lines turned out to be a nice compliment.

The caning on the flotation foam brings a tropical feel. The transom shows how the side panels overlap.

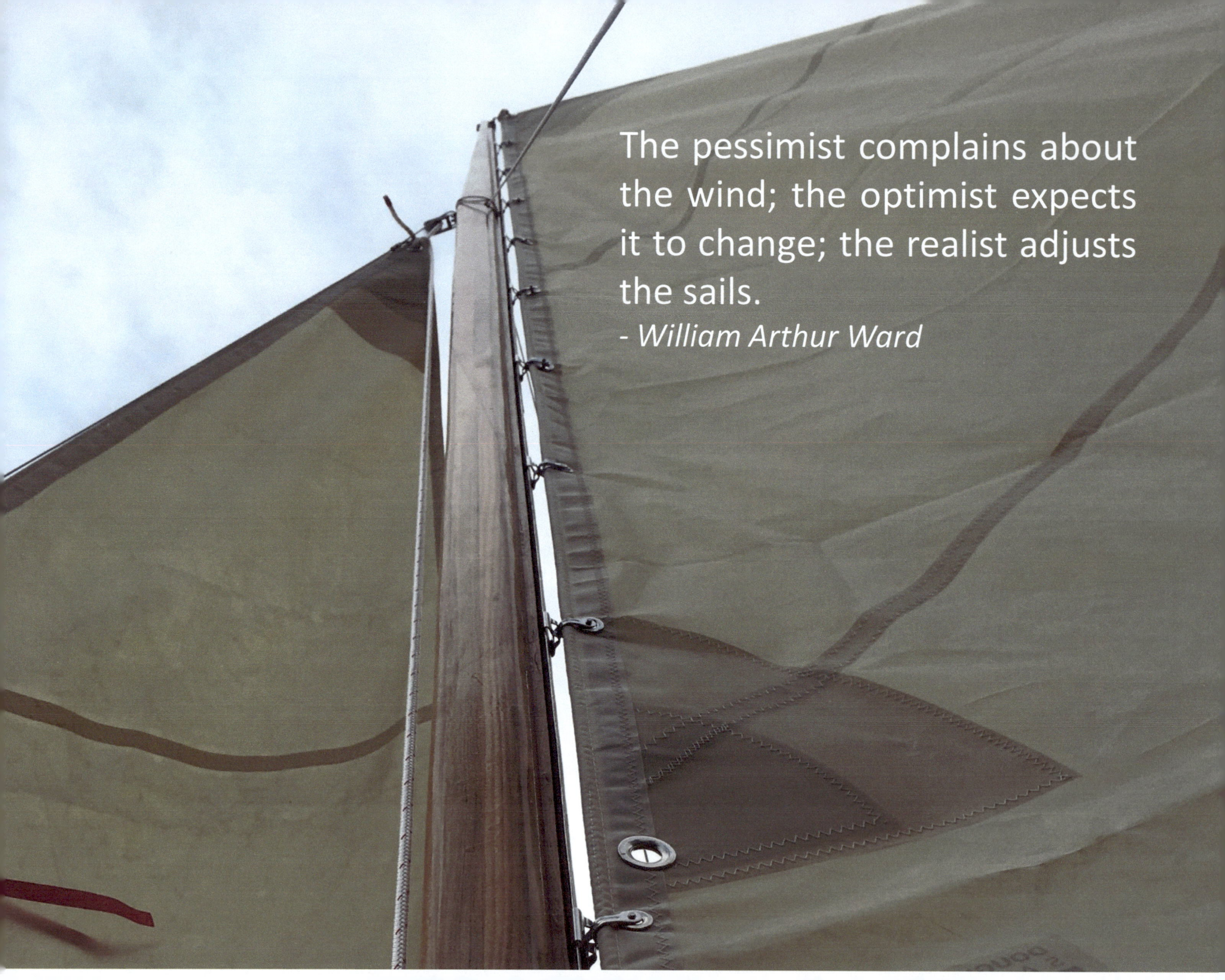

The pessimist complains about the wind; the optimist expects it to change; the realist adjusts the sails.
- *William Arthur Ward*

After the Build - Safe Indoor Storage

A custom boat should have a custom storage solution, and this hoist system worked great. The brave installation required great care to assure that the boat would be in the air and not on the cars in the morning. The dolly below is ultra-light and disassembles in 1 minute to store flat on the wall. Notice the red canvas rudder cover in the boat.

Coconut Grove Sailing Club Presentation
Wednesday, January 11, 2017, 1930 HRS

Ahoy there! This book is based on a presentation given to the Coconut Grove Sailing Club. On a rainy Wednesday night, January 11, 2017, we were honored to share our story with 40 members of the Sailing Club. Thanks to my terrific helpers, we had great fun in sharing our tale and showing a few leftover "props" from the build. This book chronicles our adventure in the Summer of 2016.

On the evening that we shared our boat building story with the members of the Coconut Grove Sailing Club, I had my son stand next to me at the conclusion of the presentation.

I lowered myself to one knee and placed my hand on his shoulder. "What was the best part of building the boat?", I asked.

"Doing it with my daddy". Ethan responded without hesitation.

Priceless.

The next day, Ethan said, "Daddy, you got to choose what we built last time, so I get to choose next time."

I reply, "OK, what do you have in mind?"

With great certainty, Ethan responds, "A car!"

We made a boat, but we made even better memories. Who knows what's next for this family?

We offer a special thanks to all of our friends that made a difference:

Chesapeake Light Craft. www.clcboats.com

Coconut Grove Sailing Club. www.cgsg.org

Coconut Grove Sails and Canvas. www.coconutgrovesailsandcanvas.com

Crook and Crook. www.crookandcrook.com

Dynamic Dollies and Racks. www.dynamicdollies.com

Jamestown Distributors. www.jamestowndistributors.com

MAS Epoxies. www.masepoxies.com

Shell Lumber and Hardware. www.shelllumber.com

West Marine.   www.westmarine.com

An extra special thanks to George Krewson.

www.ingramcontent.com/pod-product-compliance
Lightning Source LLC
Chambersburg PA
CBHW041420160426

42811CB00104B/1822